LIVING IS WHAT I WANTED

LAST POEMS

Also by David Ignatow

Poetry

At My Ease: Uncollected Poems of the Fifties and Sixties (1998)
I Have a Name (1996)
Against the Evidence: Selected Poems 1934–1994 (1994)
Shadowing the Ground (1991)
Despite the Plainness of the Day: Love Poems (1990)
New and Collected Poems: 1970–1985 (1986)
Leaving the Door Open (1984)
Whisper to the Earth (1981)
Sunlight: A Sequence for My Daughter (1979)
Tread the Dark (1978)
The Animal in the Bush (1977)
Selected Poems (1975)
Facing the Tree (1975)
Poems 1934–1969 (1970)
Rescue the Dead (1968)
Earth Hard: Selected Poems (1968)
Figures of the Human (1964)
Say Pardon (1962)
The Gentle Weight Lifter (1955)
Poems (1948)

Prose

Talking Together: Letters of David Ignatow (1992)
The One in Many: A Poet's Memoirs (1988)
Open Between Us: Essays, Reviews, and Interviews (1983)
The Notebooks of David Ignatow (1973)
The End Game and Other Stories (1996)

LIVING IS WHAT I WANTED

LAST POEMS

David Ignatow

BOA Editions, Ltd. ❧ Rochester, New York ❧ 1999

First Edition

Publications by BOA Editions, Ltd.—
a not-for-profit corporation under section 501 (c) (3)
of the United States Internal Revenue Code—
are made possible with the assistance of grants from the Literature
Program of the New York State Council on the Arts, the Literature Program
of the the National Endowment of the Arts, the Lannan Foundation, the
Sonia Raiziss Giop Charitable Foundation, as well as from the Mary S.
Mulligan Charitable Trust, the County of Monroe, NY, Towers Perrin,
and from many individual supporters, including Richard Garth &
Mimi Hwang, Judy & Dane Gordon, Robert & Willy Hursh,
and Pat & Michael Wilder.

Cover Design: Daphne Poulin-Stofer
Author Photo: Christopher Conforti
Typesetting: Geri McCormick

BOA Logo: Mirko

BOA Editions, Ltd.

A. Poulin, Jr., President & Founder (1976–1996)
260 East Avenue
Rochester, NY 14604

www.boaeditions.org

CONTENTS

III

IV

I

Staying alive

Reason for living.
I don't have any.

What is your reason for not having a reason?
Is there a difference?

Are you that sour on life?
Can I separate one from the other?

What is your strategy for staying alive?
Isn't being oneself enough?

Is it worth living without a reason?
Do I have a say in the matter?

Would you prefer not to have been born?
Did I have a mind of my own then?

Would you rather be dead now?
Do I have a choice?

Then you are opposed to suicide?
Isn't living hard enough?

Then to live is to be brave and on the move.
Are you telling me?

What would you recommend for others?
Can't they make up their own minds?

Then you should be congratulated.
Have I said something exceptional?

Live to manifest

Fear is of the universe,
as is death,
as is love, pleasure,
intimacy and cruelty.

We manifest each
living as though
we have a personal stake
in these.

We are like the mountain
that manifests the earthquake
that brought the mountain about.

And the earthquake is
of the hidden plates,
heat of the fire
at the center of the globe,
as the globe is
of the big bang
that is, of those who cannot
name it other than as God,
the mystery, and we are human
and live to manifest the pressures to survive
among ourselves as consciousness.
We are human, if not perfectly so—
killing and raping
and suppressing and enslaving—
these too manifest in us
like other forces we embrace—
the storms at sea,
the lightning.

Along with our illusion

Life is god
but its powers are pure irony
of purpose: to lift us
to its level, to die,
along with our illusion
of centrality.

The irony is that without death
there could be no life.

As though life were a question

In the ripe nectarine
is the sweetness of dying
as though we had a choice,
as though life were a question
of who must live it through,
as though we understood
or were happy
to have died unexplained
to ourselves, thinking on it
just another thought
in the minds of the living
with more to do than to think
but in the doing thoughtful
of their lives, who on their deathbeds
are reduced to thought,
smelling the air
breathing in deeply.

All living is lying

All living is lying:
we are unable to say what this life is.
We speak about it in metaphors
as if it could be other
than what it is, and even of ourselves
we say we are like this or like that.

Patient we wait
so that
once dead
we'll know perhaps just who we were,
with others thinking back on us.

An epic

So I have had it all
and need only know
what goes on in death
to satisfy my curiosity
and to resolve my fears
of selflessness that death
performs.

It is the same body and mind
with which I was born
that leads me silently
to its change: hair
turning white,
movements slowed,
thinking become impersonal
as though already
detached from self.

It is an epic
each performs
unlike the audience
of Ancient Greece engaged
in it as we tell it.

Fixed or impermanent

All these objects
fixed in their places —
trees, houses, the declaration
of independence, the bill of rights,
the constitution — awaiting
an end. The earth spins as if in search
of its executioner, perhaps
a comet sent at random
by the law of impermanence,
fixed in us
like a bent tree.

Where I built my house

Does being born matter
now that I am leaving it behind? Where
is a world I can go to
other than this ground
on which I walk and where I built my house?

Am I complaining of the shortness of life?
I am, and that makes me much like everyone else.
Follow Adam, the leader, into the ground.

The living

Death provides the food:
the zebra lay on its side
clawed into silence,
the tigress on her belly
gnawing at the belly
of the zebra with bloody teeth.

And the living zebras
at a distance, heads bowed
toward the earth, eat
of the living grass.

Unless change is a language

Plants and flowers have their colors
and shapes. They sway in the wind yet
their roots support them
and they live to grow.
If they wither
it is not said
unless change is a language.

Shadows live in the sun

Shadows lie across the pavement
and trees stand over them
as if studying the forms they make.
A car drives across, then a truck
and then a person walking,
lending his own shadow.

Trees, cars, trucks, and persons
all represented.
The sun shifts and forms merge.

Later the sun will depart,
leaving the pavement a gray blank,
as if prepared for tomorrow,
if not rain.

Shadows live in the sun.
for a short time.

One small answer

I walk into the woods, subjected
to the shade, blocking the sun, chilling me.
I walk out, embarrassed at myself
to find the woods alien
that I entered in admiration
for its silence and beauty.

If I climbed to the top of one tree
for the sun, it would be one small answer
to the problem, or if I made my home
in the branches.

Calm in the form of meaning

I stare at revelry
unable to defend myself
with truth alone.

I must depart this life
calm in the form of meaning
to be found in death.

II

Thinking my father's thoughts

I am seated in my father's desk chair
at about his age, finding myself
thinking his thoughts as then:
shortly to be sent down
in a relationship with earth
close as I have lived with friends.

The thought is not nearly so comforting
and yet where else may I turn
for reassurance, earth of the magma
flow from deep center of itself.

On what kind of day will I die,
today cloudy, after rain?

My father blowing his nose

My father blowing his nose,
first placing his right thumb
against the side of his nostril
and blowing out the issue
onto the shop floor—I was horrified,
barbarous myself for having looked on,
and I could not escape. If I left,
he would not recover from the shock.

I had believed he had given up the habit.
He carried a handkerchief,
but this time drew it out only
 to wipe his fingers and his nose,
almost as an afterthought. It was
a throwback to his life in the ghetto in Kiev.

He was my task, to help him live out
his life, as he had worked for it
in this country, my birth a sign to him
of his achievement, I, as surrogate
to his wishes, shocked into recognition.

The life we led together

——For Rose

I remember a woman
who stood up from her chair
and painted life's images
in bold colors of earth and sky.
Then sat down to write
of the people
she equated as earthlings,
glad for herself
and self-contained.

Nothing awakens her.
I look on to watch myself losing myself
in memory of a woman to whom
love was meaning, leaving me
stranded in my own vanishment
from the life we led together
hand in hand
lip to lip.

Someone of the past

Someone of the past is dying in front of me,
her face immobile.
She sees herself in me, dying too.

What we know of each other is dying with us,
no one else will ever know
and still we can't convey
to one another the past events
to live them over with a change
in sight of our eternity.

Did I mean you harm
when we lived together?
Did you mean me to be a nightmare
in your life?

Hope was the happiness

A love poem to Rose
on her approaching death,
not far off. Should I die first
this will suffice.
We will lie together
buried apart, as was ordained
from the start. It has been written
and the word has gone out.

Rose, it's enough to have lived.
It is recorded for the future
without us, as we are read
and thought of, as with suffering
and hope, but always with hope
to be restored to our true life
which we looked toward
in its absence.

This is our story
and it was not all bad. Hope
was the happiness between us.

As I die in hope
that we will not be forgotten,
not so long
as this is read and pondered,
to meet again in the eyes and thoughts
of the future, our hope restored
in the living.

For my daughter

1.
I was never so happy
as when you were born.
Everything
that did not conform
to your laughter
I let go.
In your delight
I was that child.

Work became a fable
of a man surviving
for your sustenance.
I worked as a religion
of which you were the sign,
I an acolyte
in my faith in you.

2.
My daughter, we will not meet
often from now on, separated
by distance and time,
but you are close to me.

At my age our next meeting
may be our last. I'm alive
to say so.

I cared, my thought of you,
your life assured because you love.

3.
My daughter's first gray hairs
remind me of the time
I looked on mine with curiosity
at forty, her age exactly.
She is my daughter, no doubt.

We both are traveling
in the same direction
together in our separate graves.

The prize

I thought you ought to know:
In Ward 55, Building 15,
I am highly respected
and made welcome: distinguished poet,
my son in the ward boasting about me
to his friends.

When I feel neglected
by literary critics
and their magazines,
on a visit to the ward
I hear myself admired
and addressed by Blacks and Whites,
Asians and Latins,
and respectful attendants.

Vivi

Now Vivi plays the piano once again,
not upon a grand or baby grand
but on a spinet. The sound
is not the same but it is
her spirit at seventy-nine.

She's happy and that's what matters,
at last to play upon the keys.
Her youth
is now much easier
to contemplate as not entirely
lost.

Cousin Alex

My cousin Alex, tall and sinewy,
feared his father, glancing at him
for permission to be himself.

Alex would flaunt his height
in company, his father seated
in midst, saying nothing.
To Alex it was permission
to act out his pleasure in himself.

He loved his father,
in fear of not loving him.

Silent father. His many investments
secure, a silent, disinterested man,
mildly baffled by his son's timidity
toward him.

Alex, tall above the rest of us,
dominating the room,
I remember no longer seeing him
in company with relatives,
his father steadily smoking
his Turkish cigarettes
and keeping a level voice,
offering no clues to Alex's whereabouts,
no indication of concern
at Alex's absence.

Family

Caught in its web,
he surrendered to being eaten,
grateful for the love
it signified.

At fifty

There it is again,
a woman
with arms upraised,
head tilted
to a side: the invitation
to the dance.

She is not shapely
and her hair is white
but there it is again.

To contemplate a difference

Your body is not mine
and so I look upon it
to contemplate a difference
that I study to accept
in just that difference,
and yet because of it
makes a world for me
in that you're here
for the sake of difference
of which a world is made.

Love notwithstanding

I'm angry with you,
you were sharp with me,
I spoke tentatively
you retorted with heat,
I shut up
but finally quickly,
"I'll have a check for you
when next we meet." That
silenced you.
And I felt you had mistaken me
for your former love.
I saw myself in his space
and sensed you had not changed
love between us notwithstanding.

What was I to think,
loving you as I imagined you
to be, often when both of us
were free of worries? Those
were the ideal days.

Have they been hurt
in the cut of your voice?
If so, love will rise again
but not for one another
necessarily. Perhaps we'll meet
again to make each other whole
as in the past and be as we thought
ourselves to be. Love demands it.

Living was what I wanted

Did I fall in love to look back upon it
as a lesson on how not to live
if living was what I wanted?
It was what I wanted,
with pleasure in command,
and that was pleasure by the hour
with moments in between
to reflect on limits
of the mind, in conflict
with the day and with time,
the burden that one carries
into pleasure to spur pleasure,
to be reminded of what it is to live:
to be with time, with self,
with pleasure a footnote:
the lesson learned again
as pleasure beckons to one's tiredness
and revulsion from the life
despised as truth,
learned in pleasure.

I am not for living alone

The childhood seeking
the tenderness in others
as if their voices echoed
my need, while I act tentatively
touching what I may.

I am not for absolute solutions,
I am not for living alone.
I am for others good to me
as though I love each one
since I was born. I know this
to be true. I reach out purposefully.

III

Into the circle

To my friends I am in good health
and voluble, but I have moved
into the circle, after many years
in sun and shadow, having walked
as does a sightseer, in no fixed direction.

In the circle I stand looking back
on that life. I cannot leave,
nor seem to want to. As though programmed
I look out in an act of living.

Saying yes to living

Because so many of us have died,
I want to say yes to living,
to raise buildings, pave roads,
lay sewers and pipelines,
install phones and electricity
and open stores for food,
to plant trees and keep sports
going in huge stadiums,
and because death is imminent
I live to visit the grocer
and to pay my bills.

My skeleton, my rival

Interesting that I have to live with my skeleton.
It stands, prepared to emerge, and I carry it
with me — this other thing I will become at death,
and yet it keeps me erect and limber in my walk,
my rival.

What will the living see of me
if they should open my grave but my bones
that will stare at them through hollow sockets
and bared teeth.

I write this to warn my friends
not to be shocked at my changed attitude
toward them, but to be aware
that I have it in me to be someone
other than I am, and I write to ask forgiveness
that death is not wholesome for friendships,
that bones do not talk, have no quarrel with me,
do not even know I exist.

A machine called skeleton will take my place
in the minds of others when I am dead
among the living, and that machine
will make it obvious that I have died
to be identified by bones
that have no speech, no thought, no mind
to speak of having let themselves be carried
once around in me, as at my service
at the podium or as I lay beside my love
or when I held my child at birth

or embraced a friend or shook a critic's hand
or held a pen to sign a check or book
or wrote a farewell letter to a love
or held my penis at the bowl
or lay my hand upon my face at the mirror
and approved of it.

There is Ignatow, it will be said,
looking down inside the open grave.
I'll be somewhere in my poems, I think,
to be mistaken for my bones, but There's Ignatow
will be said. I say to those who persist,
just read what I have written.
I'll be there, held together by another kind
of structure, of thought and imagery,
mind and matter, love and longing, tensions
opposite, such as the skeleton requires
to stand upright, to move with speed,
to sit with confidence, my friend the skeleton
and I its friend, shielding it from harm.

My life is not mine

My life is not mine,
it is elsewhere.
I spend days and nights
thinking about it.
I don't remember,
if at all, being
separated from it.

Was I born and raised
without a life of my own?
So I would think
if I were not so unhappy
about it.

My life is a figuration
of what I have lived in
for so long it seems
I was born in want.

The world shows me its face
of change for change alone.

Identification

Already the conductor envisions my face
as the photograph in my pocket
and does not bother to identify it.
He goes down the aisle
punching tickets, his pants baggy in the seat,
a sign all is not well with him.

I should congratulate myself
that swaying subways are gone.
I can hold up a newspaper before me
and be passed by as a fixture,
as the identification photo.
The conductor in his baggy pants
rocks down the aisle to his windy vestibule.

I am important to myself

Why am I so important to myself?
I look in the mirror
and see a face like anyone's.
I'm like everyone,
but is that important?
I'm also me.
I see a difference
in that I am important
to myself first.

Others, too, see themselves
important to themselves,
because, as with me,
there is no one left
to be them after they die.
For that reason I mean
to preserve myself.

At eighty I change my view

At age eighty to discover my illusion
about living in a hothouse of flowers.
Very well, I change my view:
a continual bombardment, Serbs in Bosnia,
and, under that constant bombardment, eat,
socialize and stroll in the streets.
A citzen of the town falls silently,
shot. In front and in the rear
we continue on our stroll and chatter
among ourselves, because, like good people,
we have adjusted
and carry an umbrella in the sun.

Make of me its purpose

Let the sun be the creative one
and make of me its purpose
of which I know nothing
except its aging me
as if I knew that being creative
is its aim, that is,
if the sun knows, if at all.

I accept

I accept the sun and the moon
to which I am related.

Atlas

I never asked for it,
strange to find
one's shoulders weighted down
in sunlight.
Can't raise my head
without everything
above me tottering
about to fall. I
shrink into myself.

Apparently I was not meant
for happiness. Burdened.
Without it, ill at ease.

Stones will pay me heed

What has brought me to you, stone,
when nothing in you can express a thought
or emotion? On the surface you are
what you really are, hard without shape.
Still, when I look I think of weight,
of crushing power.

                    This dialogue
between us is one-sided, of necessity.
I give you the power to suggest
to me my own thoughts, but I cannot
let it rest at this, that I make up
my world, of my own need. Stones
are here and they will pay me heed.

Presence in an empty room

I must accept aches and pains of the body
if I am to accept
my presence in the empty room,
with no motive for being
in an empty room, and so
with no motive for being. If
I can accept aches and pains,
I exist.

Meat is my comfort

With my mouth full of meat
I am farting with pleasure
unable at last to speak.
Meat is my comfort;
it fills the gap
of sitting at a desk
to scribble
on prepared forms
eight hours a day
after which I get up
to rush home
by train
to sit still again
reading a newspaper
reporting on the death
of someone like myself
who has gone mad
and torn up his prepared forms
and dived out of the window
like a bird
delirious,
freed of beliefs.

Out of focus

There is a sense in which living itself seems a form of suicide acted out over the years. We start with expectations only to discover we are in conflict with ourselves, carrying this negative with us. It is as if we have committed suicide already yet persist in walking about attending to our affairs.

Joy of flight

Think of this:
You on a roof
of a tall building
on fire
no help in sight
none expected.
It is happening
in a country
strange to you.
The impulse to leap
is like the joyful love
you have often flown with
in a dream.

The fire approaches
from beneath the roof,
the roof cracking.
In joy of flight
you step out upon the air
in memory of your dream.

A sound like any other

I once thought a low chord
of a trombone meant an ominous event
in my life. Now I recognize it
as a sound like any other: a truck
starting up in low gear at a street corner.

Nevertheless, I was born to
terror, remorse, pleasure and triumph.

It's my life

He is lying on the ground, twisting,
plainly in agony.
Someone kneels to ask gently
if he needs, and wants, help.
He replies, shouting in his agony,
No. Is he enjoying it? he is asked
skeptically, and he shouts,
It's my life!

He turns harshly on his questioner:
What keeps you from pain?
And the questioner, astonished,
tumbles out an answer, But I am in pain,
seeing you in pain.

You are robbing me of my life.

My wholeness is dependent

I am an electric bulb and shine when turned on, but dull and
useless in the daylight. Either condition is my natural one.
I do not choose and would not choose if I were asked. Is it
not a fact that both originate from the same source and that
one could not exist without the other, and that the prime
condition for the existence of either state is my presence? I
embrace both yet am whole. In fact, my wholeness is dependent
upon both states existing.

The live match

I lit my stove and shook the match to blow out the flame. I shook it again and a third time and noticed, curious, that what routinely happens did not. The flame persisted. Again it refused to be extinguished. This time I placed the match under a running faucet and still the flame persisted. I knew now I had a phenomenon in my hand. There was danger and I thought of what to do to keep the situation from growing critical.

It was hilarious to the firemen to be told I could not extinguish a match. Apparently, however, curiosity won out, perhaps they thought of me as a firebug to be investigated.

Holding the match between two fingers, at a distance from me, I waited their arrival, as I looked steadily at at the flame with dread and wonderment. The match was not consumed. Taking it from me, the firemen dropped it to the lawn and stamped on it. The flame continued. The firemen looked at each other apprehensively. I felt strangely vindicated.

It was understood between us silently that something was amiss, and it was dangerous, as I had earlier surmised. The live match lay there on the lawn, as the firemen formed a circle and consulted among themselves privately, confronted by a mystery. A mild breeze rolled the match towards my house. The lawn, as the match raveled throught the grass, began to burn. They attached a hose to the water pump and directed the stream but the flame persisted. The flame was licking at the walls of my house. They aimed the stream at the wall already beginning to smoke. In panic, the firemen rushed indoors and placed a phone call for more help, but by then the house with all its furnishings, including my clothes, books, correspondence, mementos, were going up in flame.

The mild breeze lifted bits of burning wood to the house next door. Other bits floated on to houses farther down the street. Nothing was in sight to help, at least to retard the fires. It was not long before our village was on fire, from house to house, and now the breese was carrying flaming bits to the next village, fire slowly expanding toward the horizon.

Everywhere people were in an uproar, their homes, businesses, cars, stores consumed. They watched burning pieces of wood sail over their heads towards an ever-widening disaster.

How were we to survive? I found it too horrifying to contemplate. The flames that began with the match were sweeping through the country and soon the entire state and nation in strong currents of upper air with nothing in their path to stop them, then carried on trade winds overseas.

The flames began to eat the earth itself, sending rocks and soil into the air in fiery chunks. We were being dispossessed of the earth itself beneath our feet, and eventually would fall into space, body by body, sailing off into the void to become as once we were, atoms or nuclei, as if we had completed our function on earth and earth itself finished with sustaining us. Together, with our planet, returned to our origins for perhaps yet another role, one not in our power to choose or know.

IV

Born to know suffering

I was born
unlike Whitman
to tears,
to know suffering,
as who has not,
but I kept at it.
And in old age
suffering is next to godliness,
because the world
is receding, it seems, not me.

                          I know
where I am headed,
in one directon, firm
in my intention, giving myself over
as to a mission in life
as I was not capable of until now,
except this last
that I can welcome with folded arms.

The flame lights up

Mistakes are many,
but it turns out
you can put them together
as you would a kindling pile
and set a match to it.
The flame lights up
the silence around you.

Something hopeful

I want to write
so that I can say
something hopeful.

Can this be it,
just this saying
that I'm trying?

This must be it
and to keep saying it
as if effort spoke
for what was not there
but insinuated
in the effort.

The old poet

I.

He has nothing more to say. From his window he looks out upon people walking past his apartment house, and that's all he can see — nothing to get excited about — to start a poem: people on their way home or to restaurants or to shop or to work or to girl or boy friends. And yet and yet, if something were there he would know or sense it: perhaps someone on the way to rob, cheat, kill or swindle.

That should start a poem. But not really. It's too common. What more is there to say about another robber, killer, swindler or cheat? Poetry needs surprise. But if not about people, who else then? How about oneself?

What does he know about himself that surprises him or that would surprise him to discover? He eats, sleeps, goes about his business like everyone else. He is even capable, like everyone else, of robbing, killing, swindling or cheating, given the right circumstance, or, as has been common among poets lately, of suicide.

He has no motive for killing himself, although he feels himself empty. Nothing any longer shocks him about himself or about others. He is just another human.

Perhaps it calls for celebration, all together in common pursuits, with death a factor. Being ordinary has its comforts, to see oneself in everyone else. It makes for a world of its own, and perhaps they sense it, walking together: their way of being that to them, at least, is of importance.

This could be their poem, made of them in the mass, without words, living it as does a poet writing his poems but bearing in mind the thieves, cheats, killers and swindlers, walking with them, shoulder to shoulder.

2.

This room is me, its breakfast table and wicker chair up against the curtained window. On the right stands my radio on the sound box of the record player across from my bed. On the left stands a television set, its back against shelves of poetry. All this is my creative self.

I sit at the table facing the window after breakfast, a manuscript lying before me. At my back is the refrigerator and above the electric stove on the washstand my cabinets for food, vitamins and prescriptions for my illnesses—all that makes it possible to continue in my role as poet.

Also at my back, as I sit at the table, is my desk, oddly enough one side up against the refrigerator, as if each relied on the other in a function important to each.

As I look down the corridor from my seat, I see my wardrobe on the right and the door to the toilet on the left. Directly ahead in the corridor is the door I keep closed to keep my privacy, on the other side of the door the accoutrements of marriage. In my room I am identified to myself, when I return to it after a long voyage to other rooms I return to myself. Is this enough for me? I must answer honestly No. It is a stopgap to my sense of an elsewhere existing within me. And when I write it is to draw this elsewhere in so that I may possess it as I possess myself, this room, to make of elsewhere another self that can exist as I exist in this room.

Can I write my way back to make of privacy many rooms for my habitation, lonely no more? But as I think of it, it is happening, and my typewriter can be heard in all the rooms.

3.

This morning, suddenly, I felt I was living out a term, and seemed strangely freed, clean of encumbrance and belief. And now I could face myself with a certain confidence, to exist free of meaning. I was value in being.

I could turn to others as I did to myself. We looked toward the stars. We could add ourselves to the gathering in the darkness of space, dark to our senses, not knowing our sources, yet because together with the planets and stars and darkness of space, we occupied the universe.

What other than ourselves occupied the universe? It was not to be seen, touched or heard from. Then we and all of which we were made that floated free — that was the universe, in death returning to the source of ourselves of which we were the source itself. It was something to know. Death was not death as once I believed but recreation of the universe. Death renewed the universe, I playing my aged role. This was my religion.

How I learned to be with others

What I thought I was writing—
for the social good—turns out to be
for my own enlightenment;
no one is listening,

True I was born alone
but I had parents
who held me in their arms.
That is how I learned
to be with others.

My parents buried,
I stand at their graves
expecting they will make themselves present.

It was never well between us:
I had poetry in mind,
they lived to earn a living
and prosper.
At breakfast we met around the table.
It was solace of a kind.

Later I in my room to read and write,
my mother to shop,
my father to visit his brother
on matters of finance.

Eventually, I occupied my own space,
free of the differences with my parents
and I realized I was alone.

Nothing I now write has this sense
of being heard, the silence I write in
is the silence I am addressing,
seeking the closeness I miss
away from home.

I married as a solution,
had children. I
continue alone.

My parents' death took with them
my one experience of community.
All other efforts have been just that:
efforts not born into.

To be a poet

Ways to die: by slashing your throat, cutting your wrists, hanging the body by the neck, stabbing, shooting, choking, car crashing, drowning yourself. There are many more, but don't bother, being busy otherwise.

One more is to be a poet. You write to free yourself of your life and write for many years, living and dying alternately.

It's surely productive of poems which, like turds left behind, mark your progress toward a perfected death.

All these signs of having escaped your life encourage others and that is another reason for writing, to invite them to an experience that needs an audience that wishes to die with you as they read. Like you, they will rejoice in keeping house and job, tokens of their strength to exist in two worlds.

It will be a time to celebrate, the world flocking to participate, an audience leaving living behind to invest in dying within the poem, and, when the last one is written, order your headstone, your last effort at freedom.

Life in the volcano

The language of life
is in the volcano.
It pours over us
in its path to create
new ground
where others after us
will walk in thought.

Where if not in words

In your basement lies a drunk, dead,
in torn, smelly clothes. You describe
his gaunt, blood-mottled face, his bitter jokes,
his bravado when confronted. He loved
his wife, so he said, his children thought
he could have been a great father.

You know as well as he that nobody
in the past compelled him to live.
He loved himself drunk.

Give him his due as a failure
who in your poems mirror
his suffering and contempt, derision
more accurate, of what we think is the good.
He is the subject
of your well-ordered life —
if you admit your unease, your insecurity
in love, your unhappiness.
You work to escape but where
if not in words limiting, addictive?

I'm not yet convinced

I'm not yet convinced that I have to die.
What proof am I looking for? A cough,
a heart pain, a sudden drop in energy,
disinterest in life, a turning away
from beauty I would have exclaimed on
in my youth?

It's not easy for me to die
as it is for some people
who limp all the way to the grave.

I mean not to die in advance of its happening.

You reading this now that I am gone,
of course, I expected to die
but while writing I was engaged
in a form of existence that appealed
to me. So here I am,
my pen in hand writing, thinking,
pleasing myself and you, I hope,
reading this. It too is living
and I share it with you in my grave.

Friendship enough

What shall I write, except that I'm unable
to tell myself what it is, and that is
where I leave it as I leave the room.
I leave behind a mysterious friend
who won't talk but will stay
and keep me company. I can write
about it and that should prove
friendship enough between us.

The spirit may enter

Each morning you write to create an other
than the tone in which you brood.
Your pen describes a door
through which the spirit—
it is a spirit—may enter
and dance before you
like a flower, neither brooding
nor distracted, knowing nothing
of death or of its own life
as a flower.

Circling the silence

I once thought I had something to say.
I said and looked
for what I had intended to say
I had not found the words.

I circle around the silence,
comparing it to death
but it is not that either
because it is tense in me,
an incitement.

I write to awaken the silence,
to acknowledge I have nothing to say,
and it is satisfying
as if having written the poem.

Acknowledgments

Grateful acknowledgment is made to the editors of the following journals where some of the poems in this book first appeared:

"All living is lying," "The old poet," "Where I built my house," "Where if not in words," in *Descant;*

"The living" in *Southern Humanities Review.*

～૭

Publisher's Note

This book of David Ignatow's last poems, most of them written in 1996, the year before his death, was edited by Virginia Terris, and by Jeannette Hopkins and Yaedi Ignatow.

～૭

About the Author

David Ignatow is the author of eighteen volumes of poetry, including this volume, and three books of prose. In a career spanning more than fifty years, he received the Bollingen Prize, two Guggenheim fellowships, the Wallace Stevens fellowship, the Shelley Memorial, the award from the National Institute of Arts and Letters "for a lifetime of creative effort," the Robert Frost Award, the John Steinbeck Award and the William Carlos Williams Award.

Born in 1914, Ignatow was raised in Brooklyn, and attended public schools there until 1932, when he entered his father's bookbinding business. In 1964 he was poet-in-residence at the University of Kentucky, followed by similar appointments at the University of Kansas and Vassar College. He was professor of English at York College, City University of New York, and also taught at Columbia University. He was poetry emeritus of the Poetry Society of America from 1980 to 1984, and poet-in-residence at the Walt Whitman Birthplace Association in 1987, serving on its governing board in 1989. David Ignatow died at his home in East Hampton, N.Y., on November 17, 1997, at the age of 83.